BASICS

DESIGNING
WITH WATER

\\ AXEL LOHRER

BASICS

DESIGNING
WITH WATER

BIRKHÄUSER
BASEL·BOSTON·BERLIN

CONTENTS

FOREWORD

We travel far to marvel at Niagara Falls, one of the natural wonders of the world, or to admire the animated fountains near Tivoli. We follow brooks and creeks to their sources and, after a mountain hike, cool our arms in wooden fountains. There are many ways to experience the spectrum of water, and design can provide a wide range of nature-oriented elements as well as artificial or artistic waterscapes.

Examining designed water installations more closely shows that they are usually the element that lends flair to a site, that reflects cultural import, gives a site its prestigious character, or perhaps just provides a playful aspect.

Creating an outdoor water design presents specific challenges regarding space, function, concept, and technical construction. As planners, we study the different ways of dealing with water more closely. Ideas and design solutions can be easily integrated into a concept. However, when it comes to the actual planning, creating the design in proportion to the space, choosing materials, or calculating load capacity and durability, quickly challenge one's knowledge.

This was reason enough to launch the series of "Basics" books on landscape architecture with this subject. The series aims to present the topic to first-semester students of landscape architecture in a straightforward, easy-to-understand manner, to highlight the essential elements, and awaken the desire to know more.

The author guides readers through the entire range of the subject of water and its design possibilities. The fascination with water is presented as a basic element that oscillates between magic, recreation, and technical challenge. The specific approach to site, developing the design, finding the formal language, and correct materials are also discussed. Technical details are addressed in the chapter "Technical Parameters." The chapters are accompanied by visual examples and diagrams that serve as tools to help one develop a design solution. The book provides useful tips and notes for a better understanding of the topic, and for practical application. This all leads to a successful design!

Cornelia Bott, Editor

INTRODUCTION: THE DIVERSITY OF WATER

Landscape architecture is a rich and complex discipline. As well as being capable of creating architectural forms and structures from natural elements, it also employs the almost infinite range and diversity of nature, which is associated with immanent mystical power and holds a deep-rooted fascination.

Water has a unique position among the natural elements. The relationship that humans have with water is complex, ambivalent, and ever oscillating between too much and too little. Water is the foundation of life. Its energy, healing qualities, light, and meditative inspiration is captivating for us all, yet water also contains an element of danger. It can instill fear and awe, and drought or floods can also kill.

Working with water as a design element has involved and always will involve this field of conflict, while still flirting with the evocations, memories, or technical possibilities that water brings.

Untamed nature

Water represents untamed nature and therefore absolute purity, freedom, and infinite power; it symbolizes the opposite of a world that is fettered by technology. These issues can be expressed dynamically in the form of roaring waterfalls, powerful animated fountains, or dense mist sculptures.

Magic

Water is both dead matter and the symbol of life. It is a fundamental part of mythology and the philosophy of nature. In many parts of the world, it plays a vital role, especially where human survival depends on solving problems of water. Images of water as a magic or animated element appear in legends, songs, or symbols and can be evoked conceptually in water designs, or by adding sculptural ornaments.

Purifying relaxation

Water is also related to cleanliness because of the role it plays in washing and bathing. This can be seen in many elements based on religion, such as baptismal fonts or the fountains located outside mosques. In small footbaths, natural swimming ponds, or ornate thermal baths, water is synonymous with relaxation, play, and sport.

Image and representations

Water is also the key to wealth and power, to the extent that it can even develop into a symbol of power above and beyond the design context – as demonstrated by the ornate fountains at the foot of Roman aqueducts, the great water axis in Versailles, or the imposing river dam project in

China today. Water can be prestigious or symbolic, depending on how it is applied as a design element. Market fountains define the center of a city; shopping centers lure customers with playful water features, and waterfalls cascading down the facades of office complexes signal the importance of the institutions within.

Technical challenge Developing solutions to technical challenges over the centuries, such as the basic water supply needed to build transportation routes or to prevent disasters, has led to a growing, substantiated knowledge of water management. Depending on the specific local challenge, there are natural aspects and site-specific technical resources, such as fountains, cisterns, or flood control structures, which can serve as technical models for designing with water.

Designing with water is always set before a diverse and complex backdrop. It references a broad range of forms, movements, and techniques, and plays with phenomena, myths, and images, thus allowing fantasy and creativity to flourish. However, the end result is ultimately what matters, that is, how well it functions as an architectural element and how it manifests the diversity and fascination of water.

Tab.1:
Examples of water elements

Type	Free elements	Recurring elements
Jetting water	Spring	Fountain
	Geyser	Water jet
	Waterfall	Cascade
Flowing water	River	Canal
	Brook	Ditch
	Runlet	Channel
Still water	Lake	Basin
	Pond	Sink
	Pool	Trough
	Puddle	Bird baths

THE FLOW OF WATER – MODELS AND EXAMPLES

Water is a much-loved design element, which can be developed in a variety of ways. This is demonstrated by an almost infinite number of designs and realized examples that reflect either the inspiration of natural landscape or artificial technological methods.

Water is in constant natural flow. Water elements can be typologically classified and their possible applications best clarified by defining various types of flow according to their character – jetting, flowing, still, and disappearing. › Tab. 1

JETTING WATER

Jetting water can be designed in a natural manner in the form of springs, geysers, mist fountains, or waterfalls. For a more artificial approach, walled fountains or large animated fountains can be used. › Figs 1, 2 and 3

The amount of jetting water is an essential part of any design concept. Other vital aspects include

_ the amount of jetting water pressure (for example a trickling runlet or powerful geyser);
_ the volume of water (a narrow pipe or rushing waterfall) and the number and direction of the sources (the single, straight line of a jet of water, or an animated fountain that covers a larger area);

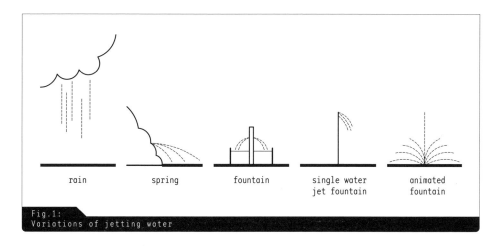

rain   spring   fountain   single water jet fountain   animated fountain

Fig.1:
Variations of jetting water

11

Fig.2:
Water gushes in a natural manner from between two stones.

Fig.3:
Jetting water with ground-level fountains and timed movement intervals

_ the outlet's design (a small slit between stones or a beautifully forged fountain pipe), and the direct environment of the spring's source (a water source with plants or an artistically designed basin);

_ the planned intervals (a constant flow or a timed, rhythmic accentuated appearance).

\\ Example:
One example for a minimalist design using jetting water is ground-level fountains without aboveground water basins and no visible components when not in operation. Stauffenegger + Stutz used this principle to design a water sculpture for a previously empty square in front of the Bundeshaus in Bern. Each of its fountains represents one of the Swiss cantons, and the sculpture's lithe, upward stream-like movements and timed dance sequences create impressive images (see Fig. 3).

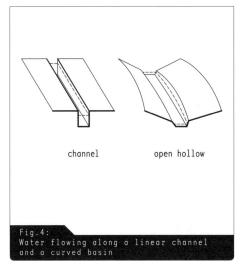

channel   open hollow

Fig.4:
Water flowing along a linear channel
and a curved basin

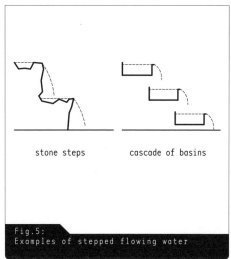

stone steps   cascade of basins

Fig.5:
Examples of stepped flowing water

Jetting water brings a fleeting image associated poetically with the naïve or childish, but also with virile buoyancy, lithe movements, lively sound, and tangible freshness.

Elements containing jetting water emphasize a point in space (for example a market fountain or a water trough near the entrance of a house), and usually create a unique space-filling character.

FLOWING WATER

Flowing water moves along longitudinal containers or in a sequence of cascading water basins. These may be landscape-inspired, such as gentle grass-lined basins, winding brooks, or stone stairways flowing with water. Artificial elements include channels, canals, or water cascades.
> Figs 4 and 5

Possible design elements include

- _ the volume of moving water, meaning the width or height of waterways and their associated speed of flow;
- _ the direction of flow and how this is interrupted (for example, by straight channels, additional basins or dams);
- _ the construction of the banks that contain and direct the water.
  > Fig. 6

13

Fig.6:
"Natural" flowing water in a grassy basin with small gravel stones

Fig.7:
Narrow water canals flow through stone slabs.

Narrow banks covered with grass are visually subtler and allow the eye to focus more on the water's movement. Wide walls or rough gravel borders (such as loose rock fill or gabions, that is stones contained in wire mesh cages) make a clearer visual impression, accentuate the force of water, and can create a rustic aspect that grows with the size of the stones used in the design.

Flowing water in brooks or cascades convey an image of complete vigor. The movement, its interruptions, and changing speed of flow is always surprising and, for this reason, attractive to the eye. Rushing, gurgling, and splashing creates a pleasantly bright, yet gentle sound.

Most importantly however, flowing water allows linear elements (such as water channels) to develop; it connects two points in space (in the case of canals or brooks > Figs 7 and 8 and emphasizes topography (for example with waterfalls and cascades).

STILL-STANDING WATER
Still-standing water requires a hollow vessel or a drain-free, horizontal basin. These can be developed as an open landscape concept, for example in the form of shallow ponds, basins, or lakes, or in more geometric, architectural forms such as bowls, basins or sinks. > Fig. 9

Fig.8:
A water canal as a sequence of stepped water basins

Various design possibilities could include

_ how the borders are developed (for example ground-level transitions or steps to sit on);
_ together with vegetation (completely bare, with a bordering cane break, or lush water lilies);
_ the use of lighting and its reflective qualities.

Still water reflects the sky, catches the light and shimmers. It can also absorb light, giving the impression of depth. › Chapter Design approaches, Sensory experience

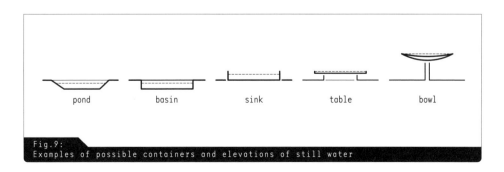

pond   basin   sink   table   bowl

Fig.9:
Examples of possible containers and elevations of still water

Still water expresses an inner quietude and powerful calm. It has the ability to captivate the viewer, convey something of its stillness, and inspire meditation.

Movement on the water's surface caused by wind or other external factors produces a subtle pulsing sound and a rhythmic beating of waves when they hit the perimeter or other architectural fixtures.

Still water can also architecturally mark the center of a room (for example, a reflecting basin of water in the middle of the ground floor of a building); it can clarify borders (castle moats), or serve as a subtle orientation system (a lake as a point of orientation or turning point along a visitors' footpath in a park). › Chapter Design approaches, Function Concepts that employ still water usually have greater space requirements than those mentioned above.

› ℘ › ℘

DISAPPEARING WATER
Disappearing water is the last section of the circulation of water. Water can disappear through drains, for example, or evaporate from impenetrable surfaces with the wind and sun, sink into porous ground, or evaporate into mist.

Design options include

_ the different possibilities of flow (decorative grates or water chutes that magnify sound); › Chapter Technical parameters, Water inflow and outflow
_ the interplay between time and speed (fleeting reflecting ponds on asphalt or water slowly dripping through a sand filter);
_ in the fortuitous and ephemeral (mist fountains or evaporation).
   › Chapter Technical parameters, Movement

℘

\\Example:
In Basedow Landscape Park, Germany, Peter Joseph Lenné is working on a small body of water in the middle of a visual axis with slight pavement widenings along the banks. The green areas and trees intermittently conceal the overall picture; the expanse of water seems larger and surprises the viewer with ever-changing forms and depths (see Fig. 10).

Fig.10:
A landscape park with a long body of water with many small inlets

Fig.11:
A geometric pool of water surrounded by hedges and forest

Concepts that include evaporating water can possess a unique allure. They envelop exotic plants in wafts of mist, form ephemeral labyrinths, encase exhibition spaces in temporary, impenetrable whiteness, or create traversable clouds that float above lakes or ponds. The works created in this manner are unique and fascinating because they recontextualize familiar phenomena and give them new dimensions.

Works incorporating evaporating water are less common. They are generally very fragile, their form and range vary greatly, and their behavior is difficult to predetermine. They are often little more than experiments, which is why they are almost never seen in public space, but this aspect, as

⌕

\\ Example:
In the park of Vaux-le-Vicomte, France, Le Notre places a free-standing water basin in the middle of a clearing surrounded by hedges. The formal reduction focuses on the light and shadow play of the trees, the changing shimmer of the water's surface, and hence the contrast between deliberate placement and surrounding nature (see Fig. 11).

Fig.12:
A reflecting pool that intentionally
has no center

well as its very melancholic moment of vanishing, possesses a particular
allure that is worth discovering and designing.

ADDITIONAL ASPECTS

The element of water is not limited to these four options, but can
also be developed in combinations (for example, in excavated springs that
flow into a stream), or using specific aspects.

Absent water

The absence of water is one example. It can be demonstrated by an
obvious "absence," for instance using structures and materials that are

\\ Example:
In Steinberger Gasse in Winterthur, Switzerland, artists Thomas Schneider-Hoppe and Donald
Judd are working on a series of simple, circular fountain basins. They play with flowing
and disappearing water in a reduced and very
precise manner, and surprise the viewer with a
reflecting pool with no center (see Fig. 12).

Fig.13:
A recognizable "absence" of water in a dry canal bed

Fig.14:
Symbolic presentation of water using raked gravel

directly related to the existence of water (e.g. stone settings or a dry river bed). › Fig. 13 It can also be suggested symbolically, with natural elements (for example by raked areas of gravel › Fig. 14 or fields of billowy grass) or by abstract means (for instance glimmering solar panels or black asphalt surfaces).

Absent water can evoke clear and alluring images that are often contemplative, peaceful, and meditative in character.

Using absent water as a design element is recommended for installations that will be unused for extended periods of time (due to weather

\\ Example:
There are beautiful examples of stone gardens in Japanese garden design, in which balanced stone settings ("islands and banks"), cut tree and hedge sculptures ("forests and solitaires"), and areas of wave-patterned, raked gravel ("water surfaces and surf") suggest dry, nature-inspired water landscapes with islands, inlets, and surf that have a reduced design, are idealized and presented in often very small spaces (see Fig. 14).

19

Fig.15:
Temporary ice skating rink on a reflecting basin in the middle of a post-industrial landscape

or limited hours of operation), or as an alternative to water if it cannot be used because of security issues or limited maintenance possibilities.

Winter aspect   The alluring effect of water can still be incorporated into the design even if the grounds remain in operation during periods of frost. White, soft, glazed frost can envelop bushes or trees; snow can partially conceal en ele-ment so that it becomes a reduced, abstract version of itself. On waterfalls or cascades, ice can develop into bizarre forms and images. A smooth, level

\\ Example:
A 12 m wide, band-like reflecting basin was realized within a robust, former industrial structure in the Zeche Zollverein landscape park in Essen, Germany. During the winter months it becomes a popular ice-skating rink with the help of adjacent cooling units (see Fig. 15).

20

sheet of ice such as those found on reflecting basins or ponds can be used for winter sports such as ice-skating or ice hockey.

Even if these are merely supplementary aspects and possibilities of use, they should still be considered in relation to the local climate, if it includes long winters. The powerful image of frozen water should also be considered from a technical perspective. › Chapter Technical parameters, Winter protection

Fig.16:
Tabletop fountain

DESIGN APPROACHES

Designing with water is a very individual practice influenced by a variety of factors. These include a specific handling of the element of water, the actual site, the role it plays as an architectural element in space, the functions the element needs to fulfill, its various sensory aspects, as well as the symbolic power that water can express.

DESIGNING WATER

Creating a design using water deals with its unique dynamism, the level of reference (or visual relationship) between the designed element and the viewer, the time-based experience, and the formal treatment of the containing borders (such as a bank or the edge of a basin).

Dynamics

The immanent dynamism – the manner and direction of movement – are the defining features of the design. According to the water's specific typology and the particular site, the designer needs to consider whether to use still, flowing, falling, or jetting water, and to decide on the appropriate liveliness, water amount, spatial distribution, or speed of flow.

Level of
reference

The level of reference – the site of an element in relation to eye level – determines how it will be experienced and therefore defines the entire

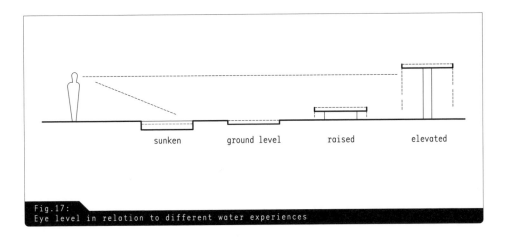

sunken   ground level   raised   elevated

Fig.17:
Eye level in relation to different water experiences

effect of the chosen approach. A low angle of perception provides a good overview. A slightly raised angle, at knee level, offers a more tangible experience. High levels of reference provide a powerful effect at a distance. › Fig. 17

Low-lying expanses of water that offer a good overall view can be used for landscaped design, in situations where meandering banks would conceal much of the actual water's surface. They can also be used in concepts that work with visibly fluctuating water levels (such as reservoirs). Sunken bodies of water have pronounced perimeters, which could appear proportionally too large for smaller bodies of water, and limit the way the water is experienced. Raising the water to ground level avoids this problem and allows subtle transitions to be created. It requires a precisely designed and constructed perimeter with little or no water level fluctuation.

Raised elements, such as basins or bowls, can present water at either a comfortably accessible height of between 0.40 and 1.20 m › Fig. 16 or raised above eye level (over approx. 1.60 m). Due to the flat perspective and foreshortened distortion, a raised body of water seems smaller than one positioned lower. Raised elements reveal the sides and sometimes, depending on their height, the undersides of their support structure, and thus require additional design considerations of formal aspects, material, ornamental features, or the type and amount of water overflow.

Using jetting water, such as a single water jet fountain, can emphasize specific aspects by the added effect of distance, which provides a better visual experience.

Fig.18:
Installation with intervals of
temporary "rain"

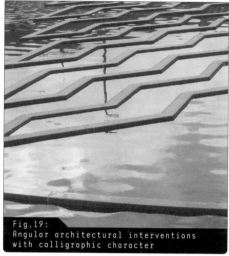

Fig.19:
Angular architectural interventions
with calligraphic character

The experience of time

The levels of reference can be devised structurally in a timed sequence, for example with lakes of still water. Moving water offers the opportunity to develop and stage other levels of perception and temporary aspects. Spatial distribution, intensity, or timed water action › Fig. 18 can develop alternating, ephemeral images. › Chapter Technical parameters, Movement

Basin

Choosing between a natural or artificial basin is directly related to the focal point of the design. With water, this can involve light, movement, or depth, as with a reflecting pool or a freestanding single jet fountain. However, it can also develop out of the related context, the contrast and dialog between water and architecture.

With the exception of mist fountains, water can only be developed together with a basin element (such as a cistern, a collecting basin, or invisible narrow channels), and its shape plays a large role in the overall character of an object. › Chapter Technical parameters, Designing the perimeter Examples can be seen in elements and structures › Fig. 19 placed in the body of water, in ornamental fountain basins, or figurative decorations. › Fig. 20

Fig.20:
Figures framing a fountain

Fig.21:
Former water clarifier in the center of
a new park landscape

UNIQUE FEATURES OF A SITE

A water design cannot be created on its own. It is one part of an architectural complex and exists within a complex spatial and thematic relationship.

The site plays a vital role in determining the effect of a designed element. The same fountain trough appears very differently from site to site – placed in the middle of a cobblestone square, in a courtyard surrounded by walls, in an overgrown bush garden, or in an open landscape. The site and its individual qualities, its overriding relationships, historical layers, and spatial formal context are essential to a coherent concept and the designed qualities of an element.

Unique features   There is great design potential in these supposed restraints. With enough financial resources almost anything is technically and creatively possible – a freedom that can result in arbitrary and interchangeable designs. It is important to search for distinctive ideas that make sense in regard to design, and not only to budget; to engage committedly with the site and its potential, and using this experience to develop individual images and sustainable technical solutions.

Overriding context   Urban structures can supply important points of reference. Significant pathways or neighboring architectural use can predetermine the site

25

Fig.22:
A large water crater with a jetting geyser

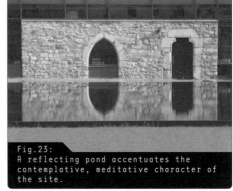

Fig.23:
A reflecting pond accentuates the contemplative, meditative character of the site.

of an element. Overriding prerequisites such as rainwater management or basic design plans begin influencing the formal outcome as early as the concept stage.

Historical layers

Structures related to former use and the visible signs of a specific memory of the topography can be additional points of reference. They provide both a very unique formal character, and the additional narrative aspect of "tracking down history." The ruins of fountains or canals can be reused, overgrown streams cleared, or historical relics such as a former industrial history can be incorporated into a new context. > Fig. 21

Spatial formal concepts

The site's spatial situation, its architectural structure and existing vegetation are the criteria for the overall design in detail.

\\ Example:
In Duisburg Nord landscape park, designed by Latz and Partner, the former clarifier of an abandoned steel works was cleaned and filled with water and blossoming cane break. Today it provides a distinctive focal point for the grounds (see Fig. 21). Europe's oldest artificial diving center with a newly built artificial underwater world is located in the nearby gasometer.

\\ Example:
In the courtyard of an abandoned industrial complex in Berlin's Friedrichshain district, Gustav Lange placed a monolithic block of limestone, laced with fine water runlets. The block's form and proportions create a clear, individual, and powerful presence in contrast with the surrounding brick facades. The still water and slow-growing moss and ferns add poetic depth and are a charming contrast to the surroundings (see Fig. 24).

Fig.24:
Monolithic limestone block laced with
runlets placed in an architectural
context

In Bad Oeynhausen, for example, powerful arrangements of water elements in space create an identifiable center point in what was once a vacant site. › Fig. 22 Their presence and beauty can echo and emphasize the language of a specific dialog, › Fig. 23 or provide their own unique response to a discourse with the surrounding architecture. › Fig. 24

Whether the formal exchange is based on a landscaped, nature-inspired discourse, or one that is more structured and architectural is influenced by context. A large, sprawling site can take a landscape-oriented response. Clear spaces, such as courtyards or other close spatial situations are more easily managed using an architecturally formal language and abstraction.

› 🔍 › 📎

📎
\\ Note:
General information and additional design ideas can be found in *Basics Design Ideas* by Bert Bielefeld and Sebastian El khouli, Birkhäuser Verlag, Basel 2007 or in *Opening Spaces* by Hans Loidl and Stefan Bernhard, Birkhäuser Verlag, Basel 2003.

Fig.25:
Modern columns as drinking-water fountains in front of a sunken pool

Fig.26:
Rainwater pipe with an added splash-
guard

FUNCTIONS

Functional requirements and specific goals can be achieved in a design involving water by using clever combinations and arrangements. In
addition to the many aspects of water supply and removal, there are also
those of recreation and sport to consider.

Drinking water

The original function of fountains was to supply drinking water. The
development of a comprehensive public drinking water system, which ultimately included individual apartments, replaced the original function of
public fountains as a town or city's water supply. Today, often filled with
industrial water, they serve purely decorative purposes. Drinking fountains are more popular in warm climates, where they are connected to the
drinking water supply and are common in inner cities or near recreation
centers and sports facilities. › Fig. 25

Rainwater
management

Precipitation that lands on sealed surfaces such as roofs or streets
needs to be collected and properly disposed of in order to protect the edi-
fice for as long as possible. Rather than directing this rainfall into the
general sewage system, it is more sensible financially and ecologically to
keep it on the ground where it fell and direct it back into the natural water
cycle by means of evaporation or infiltration. Rainwater drainage pipes are
available for this purpose, as well as collecting channels › Fig. 26 conduits,
turf troughs, › Fig. 27 ponds, or underground collecting basins. There is a
great amount of freedom regarding the integration and design of these
technical constructions in outdoor installations. These aspects of sustainable water management are particularly significant for new developments,
where a comprehensive, broad system of water management can be realized from the onset.

28

Fig.27:
Rainwater retention in a grass trough
by means of diagonally inserted sheets
of steel

Fig.28:
Collecting and warming basins in front
of densely planted fields

Irrigation

Collected precipitation and spring water can be used to irrigate gardens and plantations. Studies have shown that water that has been exposed to a few days of sunlight and is warmed by the sun is more effective for successful plant growth. › Fig. 28 The basins, troughs, and channels needed to collect, warm, and conduct water can be integrated well into the overall design and, by exploiting synergies, can often comprise the sole element of water used.

Recreation and sport

Water is very important for recreation and sport, particularly in public parks. Given the right conditions, existing elements can be developed and integrated into an outdoor installation. One example here is the English Garden in Munich. During the planning phase, von Sckell creatively integrated the existing Eisbach into his design concept by adding waves and a landscape-like course. Today, in addition to being recognized for it formal qualities, it is a popular bathing and surfing area. › Fig. 29

Even landscaped artificial bathing areas with a nature-oriented structure and water conditioning can be easily integrated into green areas. They are however only suitable for low or average operational demands. › Fig. 30 Higher usage requires reinforced basins with an electronic water conditioning system. › Fig. 31

29

Fig.29:
Surfing an artificial wave in Munich's
Eisbach

Fig.30:
Swimming pond with a artificial basin
in the bathing section

Fig.31:
Swimming pools of varying depths of
water

Fig.32:
Play area with hand water pumps, splash
grounds, and toy digger

Aquatic recreation areas work with water in a variety of forms. › Fig. 73, p. 61 They make a production of the supply of water with pumps, Archimedean screws, and waterwheels; dramatize distributing and directing water using channels, cisterns, or wind vanes; and create a design in conjunction with water, sand, and mud. › Fig. 32

Enclosures and visitor orientation

Water can also serve as an impeding barrier. Wide, deep moats such as those surrounding castles can replace walls or fences. They have a similarly obstructive function yet do not interrupt the visual relationship between different areas of the grounds. Bridges and jetties situated above

Fig.33:
A moat, together with jetties and bridges directs visitors

Fig.34:
Water wall as spatial and acoustic enclosure

bodies of water link with pathways and, together with the obstructing bodies of water, can form a planned orientation system. › Fig. 33 The center and focal points of orientation systems in historical parks or modern amusement parks are often defined by large bodies of water that sometimes cannot be crossed, such as lakes or fjords. Visitors are led along prescribed routes to significant sites and attractions.

In contrast, elevated animated fountain blocks or water walls work with obstructing views. They form a protective facade that conceals undesired functions and elements. The sound they create can pleasantly block out noise from a neighboring street. › Fig. 34

SYMBOLISM
Water is rich in symbolic value and has powerful religious roots. This phenomenon has developed over the centuries and is still true today, even if at the unconscious level.

Symbol

Depending on context, the form and movement of water can represent serenity, refreshment, vitality, or wealth. It is a cross-cultural symbol of life and temporariness. Water not only literally ensures survival; it also symbolizes human intellect and spirituality. The moon, water, and femininity are closely related in terms of symbolism.

Water in religion

All three monotheistic global religions were established in dry climates – so, naturally, nature's religious significance was closely associated

31

Fig.35:
Oriental garden with animated fountains and canals

Fig.36:
A simple fountain near a cloister

with the element of water from their very beginnings. The purifying quality of water is often glorified: in Islam in the form of a ritual ablution, or washing before entering a mosque, or in the Hindu faith by bathing in the Ganges River. Almost every Jewish community has a Mikvah, or a ritual bath with clean, flowing water. But only those who submerge themselves fully are ritually cleansed.

For a long time, the Christian faith practiced the baptism ritual by completely immersing the body by either dipping it into water or pouring water over it. In Western societies, this practice has been replaced by dripping water onto the forehead of the person to be baptized. Baptism symbolizes a devotion to Christ and acceptance into the church. It symbolizes death and resurrection. In Catholic and Orthodox churches, holy – consecrated – water plays a significant role generally.

SENSORY EXPERIENCE

Many elements possess – beyond the purely functional level – a unique characteristic to which the design should specifically respond. Vegetation, for example, can introduce the factor of time as a fourth dimension. In harmony with the seasons, plant growth and changes in colors and shape will transform the look and mood of a landscape design, year after year. Water's unique characteristic exists in the diverse ways it can be experienced with the senses.

Designing with water is more expressive if the sensory experience is integrated into the concept and recontextualized. It is difficult to say which of the senses is most or most intensely stimulated by water. But ultimately a harmonious, well-balanced interplay is the key to a successful composition.

Pure water is clear and transparent. It has the ability to capture light. Water drops, reflecting pools, and waves all become prisms in which light is refracted and fractured into an infinite diversity of shimmering sparkles. Water can be colored by sediments, solutions, or emulsions.

The addition of air bubbles makes water less transparent, and more white or opaque. The air dissipates as soon as the water settles and the effect disappears. This is what forms the white crests of waves or the soft, white water sculptures made by foam guns or "schaumsprudlers." › **Chapter Technical parameters, Movement**

Material or sediments picked up by flowing through soil or stones, for example, can also color water. The brown coloring often seen around the outlets of moors comes from the humic acid eluviation commonly found there. Colors derived from solutions are durable and remain stable for a longer period of time, but they are pale and cannot be controlled.

Wild, rapid flowing water tears sand and stone from the riverbed and propels it forward. These sediments color the water yet with little of the transparence we know from the fresh, green color of mountain streams. When the current subsides, the sediments settle and, with it, the color.

ρ

\\ Example:
Water represents life, death, and resurrection. Fountains with contained, serene designs are placed in Christian cemeteries or nearby cloisters, for example in the form of thin jets of water, stone fountains, or small labyrinthine waterways (see Fig. 36). In oriental gardens, water represents the four rivers of paradise (see Fig. 35).

Fig.37:
"Kneipp" basin with handrail and
various ground coverings

However, a body of water's "color" usually comes from its surface reflections of the surrounding environment, or from objects below the water's
surface. The way we perceive these colors depends on the angle of view and
refraction between the air and the water's surface, and from the difference
in brightness. The deeper the water, the "deeper" the color appears – an effect that is enhanced by natural deposits that form on the river's sides and
bed. The dark, almost indistinguishable floors of pond contribute to the
reflecting effect on the water's surface. Light-colored floors, such as those
in swimming pools, make the water look clear, bright, and transparent, and
decorations on the pool's floor can therefore easily be seen. › Fig. 38

\\ Example:
"Kneipp" basins are for bathing knee-deep in
cold water. The up and down movements and
alternating between warm and cold water are
known for their rejuvenating effects, which can
be enhanced by using tactile floor coverings
such as gravel (see Fig. 37).

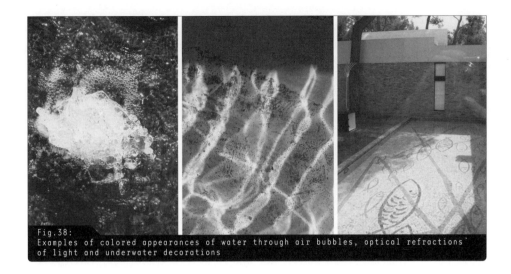

The sense of taste

Pure water does not have a flavor of its own. Eluviations and solutions from the surrounding soil or stones provide the water's flavor. Spring water can be tapped and used, for example, in drinking fountains.

The sense of smell

The "scent of water" is produced in the same way as its taste, through soluble additives or the scent of moist materials. In order to perceive the scent, aromatized water has to be released into the atmosphere as a vapor or spray. The fresh, slightly mineral scent near irregularly falling waterfalls is created in precisely this manner.

The sense of touch

Water can be directly physically tangible by diving into it, or indirectly through exposure to steam or atomization. Temperature and air humidity can relativize the effect. Atomized water, for example, is perceived as pleasantly refreshing in a dry, hot atmosphere, but in a cool, humid atmosphere it seems unpleasant, cold, and disagreeable.

The sense of hearing

The sound of water, with its highs and lows, rhythm and changing tone, reflects many musical qualities: the roar of a mountain river, the full, powerful gurgling of fountains, the muted pulsing of schaumsprudlers, or the mechanical falling of a single water drop. Pitch and sound quality depend on the amount of water, its speed and the resonant body upon which it falls. Thus, the speed of flow, the type of waterway, the shape of the

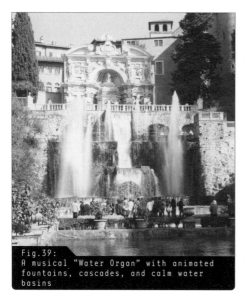

Fig.39:
A musical "Water Organ" with animated fountains, cascades, and calm water basins

Fig.40:
A distinctive setting for a water installation

fountainhead, the dimensions, height, and depth of the surface of impact, and the frequency of the pump cycle all influence the particular sound of a water installation.

> ◫ > ♀

◫

\\ Note:
Due to the number of influential factors, sound is as difficult to control as the fall of water, and should be tested and adjusted during the construction phase. This can be done by changing the impact flange (e.g. using different angles through which water enters), the resonant body (e.g. stone instead of wood), or speed of flow.

♀

\\ Example:
The many animated fountains, cascades, and water basins of the "Water Organ" in the gardens at the Villa d'Este gardens in Tivoli, Italy, are visual reminders of an actual musical instrument, while changing water pressure, the various forces of the jet streams, and the differentiated surfaces of impact serve as acoustic reminders (see Fig. 39).

TECHNICAL PARAMETERS

After finding a concept for a water installation based on the existing site and one's own individual inspiration, the designer must expand and develop the idea into a coherent and sustainable design that is conscious of the available technical and financial possibilities.

The questions and possible solutions are as diverse and individual as the chosen approach, and require the imagination and resourcefulness of the planner down to the last detail. Issues of the water's availability and source, the type of basin, the water's direction, movement, and overall scenographic design are paramount in this regard.

WATER AS SCENOGRAPHY

Source
The first thing to be established before considering a water installation is whether sufficient water in the required quality is available during the hours of operation. Water can be tapped from springs, lakes, rivers, rainfall, groundwater, or the local mains. It can then be collected in an intermediate reservoir and supplied to the planned design when needed.

Natural springs of sufficient capacity with natural outflow points are an ideal and affordable basis for a water design. Water quality is determined by the soil horizon through which it flows. Building a covering over the mouth of the spring protects it from impurities. This method can also combine several springs and, given sufficient reservoir volume, help compensate for the varying capacities of the different springs, as they often fluctuate over the year.

Water can also be obtained from aboveground sources such as streams or lakes with pipes, pumps, or water engines. Water mills, with their typical dams and tailraces, are a familiar example of this method. The procedure ensures a consistent supply, but the exiting water often requires extensive treatment.

Precipitation such as rain or snow can be collected year-round from roofs, town squares, or other sealed surfaces. The amount collected and how and when it is distributed is determined by the local climate, and can vary greatly. This can mean water supply shortages for the installation, especially in summer, or during a prolonged dry spell. The collected downfall is stored in aboveground basins or underground cisterns of the appropriate dimensions before being tapped and seasonally distributed to other uses. Rainwater is usually of high quality but can be contaminated by impurities from runoffs from neighboring sealed surfaces.

Groundwater can be found in the hollow spaces of pervious rocks and in sub-surface soil layers. It can be easily pumped from porous grounds such as gravel or sand, thus guaranteeing a consistent supply. Exposing an aquifer by large-scale excavation, as in gravel mining, creates permanent lakes of high-quality water.

A fairly simple way of obtaining water is to use the existing drinking water system. The water supply is usually consistent and of high quality and needs no additional treatment or conditioning. However, water bills can be costly in the medium term.

Depending on the design in question, it may also be possible to combine different water sources. The decisive factors include local availability of water, existing reservoir possibilities, ensuing cost, and desired quality.

> 🛈 > ✎

Structure

A water installation > Fig. 41 is supplied with water via an inflow and outflow, occasionally in conjunction with a buffering reservoir. > Chapter Technical parameters, Water inflow and outflow Water can be presented alone (e.g. as a free-standing fountain) or together with a fabricated basin (e.g. trough fountain). A basin is a concave form that is either visible (basins, bowls, or hollows) or not visible (under a grating or in sub-surface pump chambers), depending on the design. > Chapter Technical parameters, Liners and basins Additional interior hydrologic cycles can be planned for moving water (such as purifying circulations or animated fountains). > Chapter Technical parameters, Movement

Water quantity

The quantity of water required is determined by the volume to be filled (fountain basins or ponds), the concealed installations (connecting

🛈

\\ Note:

In most countries, any interventions or changes made to existing water is subject to strict laws. This also applies to the delivery or introduction of groundwater. The time needed to process requests and issue licenses is often lengthy, which needs to be taken into account during the project development.

✎

\\ Tip:

It is best to use drinking water in designs that include direct physical contact with water. Designated drinking fountains and installations, such as water play areas that invite direct contact with water, have to use drinking water for reasons of hygiene.

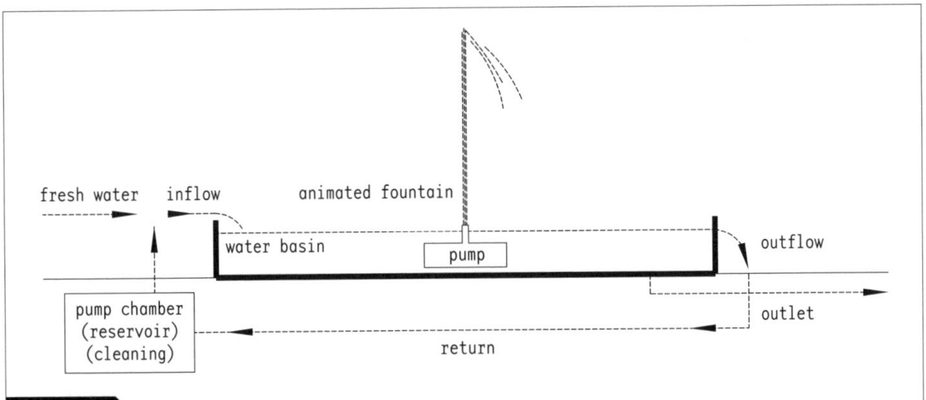

fresh water   inflow   animated fountain

water basin

pump

pump chamber
(reservoir)
(cleaning)

outflow

outlet

return

Fig.41:
The principle of a water installation

pipes or buffering reservoirs), as well as temporary quantities needed for cascades or animated fountains.

A water inflow is temporarily required to completely fill the installation, and permanently required to compensate for water loss. Loss results from regular use, for example, from spilled water, animated fountains, replacing some water in order to maintain quality, or by evaporation.

LINERS AND BASINS

Water does not tolerate errors in concept or construction. It is incredibly precise when it comes to finding the tiniest permeation, passing through it until it reaches the next impermeable area, where it stops.

> \\ Note:
> Loss by evaporation is caused by intense expo-
> sure to sun and wind. This can result in a loss
> of one centimeter per day in open bodies of
> water, even in temperate climates. To counter
> the effect, make sure there is some shade and
> protection from wind on the site you have
> chosen.

Tab. 2:
Different liners

Liners for open, landscaped designs	Liners for consistent, architectural designs
Clay/silt	In situ concrete
Bentonite	Concrete component
Flexible membranes	Plastic
Tar-bitumen roof sheeting	Steel
Mastic asphalt	Wood
Shotcrete	Masonry
Plastic	Natural stone

A correct basin or sufficiently impermeable foundation soil is rarely available. Thus, the decisive factors in a successful and durable water installation include choosing a durable liner; a precise, detailed development of the perimeter and transitions; and a sound connection between individual components.

Depending on material and construction, each type of liner is unique in character beyond its technical advantages and disadvantages, and can support the formal requirements of a concept to a greater or lesser degree. › Tab. 2

The desired look, the design context, form and dimensions, the energy of the water's movement, the way in which the body of water will be used, and finally, the soil foundation determine the type of liner required. The top edge of the liner must always be continuous and sit firmly above the desired maximum water level. › Fig. 42 and Chapter Technical parameters, Designing the perimeter

The soil foundation needs to be sufficiently compacted and able to support the weight of the future body of water. Any later resettling can result in damages to the liner and perimeter design. As a rule the following methods are used:

Clay/silt

Clay is the oldest liner method. 30 cm of clay or silt with low water permeability ($k \leq 10^{-9}$) is applied to a stone-free, stable, and profiled foundation; it is then compacted and covered with a protective layer of gravel sand. A slope of up to 1/3 can be developed using this method.

The liner layer is delivered as dry bulk, unloaded, and applied evenly. Adobe bricks and prefabricated clay elements are also good alternatives for smaller areas. They are applied in several layers and then compacted.

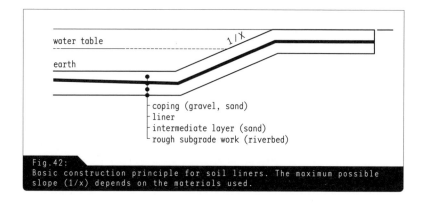

water table

earth

┌ coping (gravel, sand)
├ liner
├ intermediate layer (sand)
└ rough subgrade work (riverbed)

Fig.42:
Basic construction principle for soil liners. The maximum possible slope (1/x) depends on the materials used.

During construction, the clay must maintain the correct degree of moisture to ensure a secure seal.

The natural character of clay and silt guarantees a high level of emotional acceptance on the part of future users. The material can also be easily disposed of if the installation has to be demolished. However, if the water supply is turned off or stops, and the material is allowed to completely dry out, deep cracks can appear. These may cause permanent damage, as do heavy use or profuse root growth. Due to their swelling property, liners made of clay or silt have a self-repairing power in smaller installations. This quality, together with adding gravel and sand to fill existing small cracks, allows the material to automatically compensate for slight damage to the liner or to absorb marginal shifts in the subsoil, without additional corrective measures. On the other hand, it is more difficult to integrate or make penetrations in clay liners; these usually require additional, wide rims of flexible membrane.

This liner method suits near-natural bodies of water that are permanently filled with water, are not heavily used, and have few installed fixtures, such as garden ponds.

Bentonite

One special form of clay liner is bentonite, a highly absorbent stone made of clay minerals, which is milled into the soil level as a mealy powder before being compacted and covered with a protective layer of gravel or sand. Some manufacturers offer alternatives to the loose admixture in the form of prefabricated mats, which can be laid onto the soil.

Bentonite increases the soil's actual impermeability to water —making the ground an additional liner layer and thereby eliminating the need

41

for costly soil replacements. This is a good method if the site's soil already possesses a high level of water impermeability. Other application options and restrictions correspond to those of clay.

Flexible
membranes
This method is most common in household gardens. Plastic sheets 1.5–2.5 mm thick are cut to size and can be bonded together. They are laid on a pre-modeled, stable, fine-grained foundation ground, on top of a leveling layer of sand, and covered with a protective layer of gravel sand. Slopes of up to 1/3 are possible. Steeper slopes can result in erosion of the top layer, and gradually to exposure of the membrane due to its sensitivity to pressure and ultraviolet rays.

Natural-looking perimeters can be molded by gently warping the membrane, as can also be done with clay liners. Connections with fixtures or penetrations can be made watertight buy using flanges or terminal strips. Subsequent repairs are only possible to a certain degree.

The advantages of flexible membranes include availability, fast and easy installation, the ability to seal even very permeable foundations, and the relatively economic price.

This method is rarely used in larger technical constructions such as rainwater retention basins or designed installations for smaller landscaped pond installations.

Tar-bitumen
roof sheeting
Tar-bitumen roof sheeting as a liner is similar to the flexible membrane. The tar-bitumen roof sheeting consists of sheet material coated with bitumen on both sides. The materials needed are easily available and

\\ Note:
Check the ultraviolet and root resistance when choosing the membrane. The membrane should be lying flat and smooth without debris before applying the covering material, because this is where tears can develop. If there are plants at the site such as cane break or bamboo that have aggressive root growth and can easily penetrate the membrane, then a stronger cover, a higher-quality membrane, or additional root resistant plastic liner should be used for the vegetation area.

\\ Tip:
Piercing the stone-filled sheet asphalt for pipelines or outflows is best done by casting a flange directly into the asphalt. To connect the construction to other architectural structures, countersink a seam and seal it with asphalt. Smaller architectural elements such as stairs can be directly mounted on the liner.

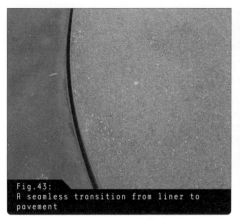

Fig.43:
A seamless transition from liner to pavement

Fig.44:
Mixed construction method with asphalt, concrete and steel

simple to use. However, they are not ultraviolet or root resistant, which means that this otherwise economic liner method can only be used for temporary installations.

Mastic asphalt

Mastic asphalt is a dense bituminous mass that is fluid when hot, and can be poured. Two 1 cm thick coats are applied to a graduated foundation ground with an anti-freeze layer, mineral substratum, and a layer of bitumen binder. This method allows for a slope of 1/2.5 and steeper. It is a durable and stable liner method and can be added to later and resealed. The procedure can only be done using the correct technique. It is a complex process and relatively expensive for small installations.

Stone-filled sheet asphalt is a suitable alternative to this method. It is more economical to produce and to install, but does not yield the same dense porosity as mastic asphalt and therefore calls for a more technically elaborate installation along the perimeters.

The stone-filled sheet asphalt liner method is recommendable for large, uneven areas, for a porous but stable foundation, and for an installation that is heavily used such as an inner-city pond installation. It allows for a smooth transition to the pavement of the surrounding pathways and can therefore be used to build shallow, traversable reflecting pools.

> Fig. 43

In situ concrete

The cast-in-place method requires the water installation to be built on a stable foundation, using high-quality, watertight cement, preferably reinforced. With the correct formwork, all slope angles and exact forms

43

can be cast on site. › Fig. 40, p. 36 Producing these components directly where they will be needed calls for a greater amount of tolerance in the original design due to the building site's unique work conditions, the specific construction of the formwork, and the shrinkage of the cement. Visible areas can be fabricated as smooth, exposed concrete, or processed as masonry, painted, or tiled.

Concrete is nontoxic and therefore safe for plants and animals. In the early stages, water runoff can alter the water's pH, but changing the water can rectify this problem.

This method is used mostly for larger architectural, geometric projects such as swimming pools, water canals or sinks, and if the installation will be used heavily. › Fig. 45

› 🗋

Concrete components

Concrete components are manufactured in a factory, delivered to the construction site, and installed on a prepared foundation ground. Large installations can consist of several components or, especially when building large base plates, can be added to on site using the cast-in-place method.

With assembled constructions, the joints must be worked and sealed with extreme care. Besides ensuring a high quality of concrete, industrial fabrication also guarantees very precise building elements, which affects dimensional tolerance as well as the way the surface can be developed. › Fig. 46

🗋

\\Note:
Concrete segments larger than 5 m require expansion joints, which can be made watertight by inserting liner tape. Since these joints influence the future appearance of the water installation, it is important to consider the design as well as the technical aspects of these sections, for example, whether or not to place the joints at regular intervals, and so on. Even after treating the surface by stabbing or elution, the reinforcements still need to be protected. For concrete hydraulic engineering constructions, a large concrete cover is recommended to protect steel reinforcements from corrosion, meaning that many constructions will need to be larger than structurally required.

Fig.45:
Trough fountain made of in situ
concrete

Fig.46:
A precision-built concrete component

The available transportation method and capacity is the only aspect that can restrict the components' dimensions and forms.

The prefabricated elements are called cast stones, and their visible surface is stone cut or designed by stabbing, granulating, sandblasting, etching, water blasting, or sanding. Concrete components are popularly used as monolithic elements or as essential components for architectural designs when high precision or a specific surface structure is required, or when large quantities have to be produced or manufactured on site, away from the construction area. This method is comparable to natural stone, but is generally more economical.

Shotcrete   Shotcrete is a specific form of concrete engineering. Special concrete in thick fluid form is delivered to the construction site in a closed line and sprayed with a pneumatic gun onto a prepared surface consisting of cast forms, soil, or other components. The impact pressure of this seals the ground soil. Reinforcements might be required, depending on how the water installation will be used and the quality of the foundation ground.

This method is recommended for installations planned for a changing topography, for installations with several links to architectural structures, or for installations that will need to withstand heavy use. It is similar to the mastic asphalt method, and can be transported by pipeline if the construction site is difficult to access.

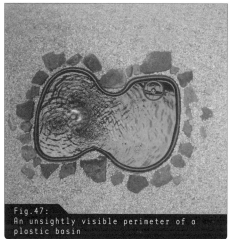

Fig.47:
An unsightly visible perimeter of a
plastic basin

Fig.48:
Plants in a steel water trough with
very thin walls

Plastic components

With this method, plastic- or fiberglass-reinforced synthetic resin is industrially manufactured in the required form and lowered on site into an excavation pit according to the manufacturer's instructions. Large basins often call for additional stabilizing backfill, for instance, of lean concrete. Plastic components are readily available for small- to mid-size installations, some of which can be reused. However, is difficult to conceal the fiberglass basin well, making it complicated to aesthetically integrate the structure with the surrounding grounds. › Fig. 47

This method is common for temporary installations and smaller decorative pools, for example, as an underground construction that is concealed by stones or fully visible as aboveground swimming pools.

Steel

Steel constructions are used for fountain installations, decorative pools, Kneipp footbaths, swimming pools, and installations that will be heavily used for long periods of time, such as dams, water chutes, or play areas. The optical litheness of steel is always surprising. › Fig. 48 It is highly durable and can be worked and installed very accurately, which is useful when building a reflecting pool according to specific, precise requirements.

As a rule, non-corrosive stainless steel is used, but this material can look sterile. This problem can be rectified by a variety of surface treatments including sandblasting, painting, or powder coating the surface. Paint will wear and peel after a period of time and become unsightly.

Fig.49:
Thick walls of steel for a fountain
with fine jets of water

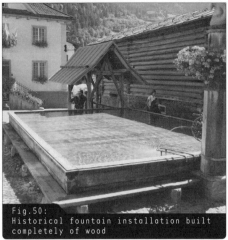

Fig.50:
Historical fountain installation built
completely of wood

Galvanized and crude steel are increasingly being used to build fountains and perimeters, as well as weatherproof construction steel, a stain-
less-steel alloy with an interesting corrosive, weathered-looking "rusted"
surface. › Fig. 49

Wood

Wood has a long tradition as water basins, particularly in forested
areas. Pipelines and troughs can be fashioned from entire tree trunks. Long,
box channels, densely placed together, is a method used to build overshot
watermills, the wide characteristic reflecting pools for wash yards, and
impressive fountain installations. › Fig. 50

These variations can be used for architectural forms and can therefore
be compared with concrete construction methods. Permanent structures

\\ Tip:
Even weatherproof construction steel will
eventually corrode if it is kept wet or is
occasionally wet over a long period. It is
recommended to design the walls thicker than
structurally necessary in order to avoid
medium-term loss.

Fig.51:
Detail of a wooden floor with a thin canal as a perimeter

should be made using strong timber that is suitable for water construction (oak, larch, and tropical woods). › Figs 50 and 51

Walled basins

Walled basins of brink or natural stone are popular in climates with mild winters. Walled constructions offer a great deal of freedom to develop form, mix materials, and design fine-structured surfaces. › Fig. 52

However, a stable substructure is essential to prevent cracks caused by movement, or to be able to use frost-resistant bricks with low porous volume to protect against cracks in freezing weather. The many joints will always present a liner problem, which can be rectified by installing a pre-fabricated concrete basin. This will however affect the appearance of the design. Walled constructions are recommended for small architectural ponds and channels.

Natural stone

Without a doubt, natural stone is the most important and impressive material for water basins, fountain stones, shells, and troughs.

One simple variation would be a supporting concrete foundation combined with a thin upper layer of natural stone. Water channels are made of curbstones, cobblestones, or rough gravel. To save material and cost, smaller fountain blocks can be faced with thin sheets of stone; yet even precise joint work and caulking does not counteract the two-dimensional, rather fragmented quality of the stone-facing method. › Fig. 53

Fig.52:
Spring basin with thin, raw quarried natural stone, laid sandstone, and surrounding vegetation

To avoid this problem, sandstone can be used to construct fountain blocks. This is a natural stone that is usually hand-processed by stonemasons. Solid, natural stone allows for a deeper sculptural treatment of the stones, which is necessary for curved and bowl-like forms, or decorative features. › Fig. 54 The joints between the stones will close and become waterproof if the stonework is executed with skill and absolute precision. Lead grouting is the most permanent method of sealing the joints.

Monolithic compositions are impressive when the uninterrupted force of stone interacts with the agility of water. › Fig. 55 Monolithic designs are contingent upon the pre-existing size of the blocks of stone, in other words, the thickness of the stone layer in the quarry, the extent to which the stone can to be processed, and transportation restrictions.

Natural stone can adapt to the slightest tolerances, so that controlling a precise flow in cascades or falls is possible even with low volumes of water. Processing the surface also enhances the overall look of the design. Ground or polished surfaces emphasize the shimmering quality of water, and accentuate form and elegance. Mottled or slightly sandblasted processes give the surface a velvety matt look that eventually weathers and becomes more interesting with age. Coarser processes such as stabbing or granulating not only give the stone a rustic appearance, but – depending upon the depth of the water – may also slow the water's flow and allow more moss to grow on the surface.

49

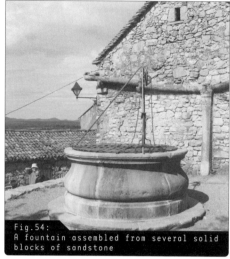

Fig.53:
A fountain block clad with thin plates of natural stone

Fig.54:
A fountain assembled from several solid blocks of sandstone

Unusual basins There is a great variety of material available for smaller installations, for objects such as fountains and troughs where the liner and form are one and the same, perhaps decoratively designed and therefore a significant part of the concept. Regional context, locally available raw materials or traditional production or work methods can be expressed in this way. Glass, terracotta, or wax › Fig. 56 can be used, as well as aluminum, cast iron, bronze, lead, and other metals and alloys.

\\ Tip:
Natural stone is subject to natural process of erosion. This is accelerated by existing pores, fine cracks, water penetrating the stone, cracks caused by frost wedging, and by tension caused by oscillating temperatures and after time, destroys the stone. To avoid this, only use natural stone with a good frost and water resilience that is manufacturer certified and guaranteed.

Fig.55:
A thin film of water flows along a
monolithic natural stone fountain.

Fig.56:
A rare example of a wax fountain in a
temporary garden

DESIGNING THE PERIMETER

Designing the water's perimeter is one of the most essential phases of creating a water installation. How it is chosen and developed clarifies the design's overall coherence. Its form – an obstructing element with vegetation or walls, or an inviting one with footbridges, stepping stones, or steps – influences the way the water installation will be used and experienced. The perimeter defines the overall character, whether natural-looking or architectural, solid or finely structured.

Location

The perimeter is usually the most sensitive area of a water installation because it is the edge of the liner layer and the transition from water to surrounding environment. For one thing, water attracts the visitor and should be experienced as closely as possible, meaning there is more impact on the perimeters – so they need to be designed and built with extreme care. For another, perimeters are constantly exposed to fluctuating water levels, moisture penetration from the soil, or a steady swell of waves, all of which need to be counteracted by detailed planning and structural precision.

Perimeters have to be consistent and at least as high as the planned maximum water level as determined by inflow and outflow, and must be perfectly fitted and integrated into the form of the liner layer. Fluctuating water levels caused by evaporation or use must also be taken into account.

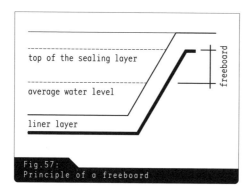

top of the sealing layer

average water level

liner layer

freeboard

Fig.57:
Principle of a freeboard

Capillary
action

Most materials have their own capillary action, a candlewick-like effect that is determined by the inner pore structure of the material. The capillary effect makes water sink into the soil beyond the visible water surface, which leads to water loss in basins, permanently waterlogged perimeters, and, depending on the material used, a decrease in the stability of the perimeter.

Freeboard

A freeboard is commonly used in perimeter design to guard against damage and water loss. This is a securing continuation of the perimeter with a liner that extends above the maximum planned water level. › Fig. 57 The freeboard's height is determined by the size and momentum of the water installation, and its exposure and use. This is less necessary for smaller features such as small water bowls or birdbaths, where moving water splashed over the sides is not a problem. With mid-sized park ponds, a 20–40 cm freeboard is recommended. For natural bodies of water, the freeboard can extend to over 1 m.

\\ Tip:
Integrating a capillary barrier in the perimeter design will interrupt the capillary effect and thus guard against water loss and waterlogging at the edge zones. Suitable options include concrete or closely laid natural stone perimeters with low pore volume, as well as loose fills of coarse gravel or gravel sand with a low fine fraction content and large pore volume.

52

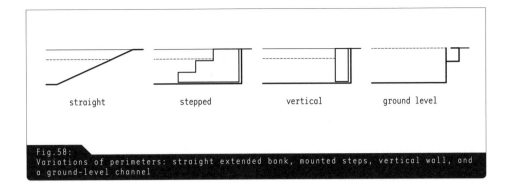

straight   stepped   vertical   ground level

Fig.58:
Variations of perimeters: straight extended bank, mounted steps, vertical wall, and a ground-level channel

A freeboard gives the perimeter a more robust appearance and creates a division between the water experience and the visitor. The water table seems too "deep" and too small in relation with the overall proportions. This impression can be counteracted by the appropriate landscaping with vegetation and a more level, yet barely visible warping of the liner layer. Adding steps that lead into the water can even emphasize this technically produced high jump.

Bank

Perimeters are developed from the liner material, and by mixing elements, materials, and methods to form a continuous, formally cohesive, and durable liner. › Fig. 58 Perimeters are vulnerable to water movement, which can cause washouts and erosion, and strain due to warming or vibrations from heavy use can produce cracks around fixtures (such as footbridges) or at the seams where the material changes.

A simple way of forming perimeters is to slowly pull up the liner (for instance, mastic asphalt or mud liners) to reach the top of the freeboard. Here, the material's possible maximum slope as well as its minimum level of stability when wet need to be considered. This method creates relatively broad banks with long, shallow water zones, but stable structures like concrete walls or packed stone allow for steeper slopes and narrower banks of deeper water.

The choice of material to be used and the course of the perimeter influence the character of an edge zone as open, landscape-oriented, or straight and architectural. › Tab. 3

Natural-looking, landscaped perimeters

Naturally designed banks have a fluctuating interplay of water depth, perimeter width, materials, and plants and therefore need a perimeter that is varied and diverse. The irregular appearance allows a high level of

Tab.3:
Overview of perimeter coping materials

Recommended materials for open, landscape-oriented perimeters	Recommended materials for straight architectural perimeters
Grass	Walls
Hedges/bushes	Stairs
Gravel and sand	Channels
Packed stone/rock	Gabions
Wicker	

flexibility when choosing the type of liner › Chapter Technical parameters, Liners and basins the edge zone's form, the subtle integration of a freeboard, or when creating the correct habitat for the perimeter's vegetation. › Figs 59, 60 and Chapter Technical parameters, Plants

Structural, architectural perimeters

Hard-edged, architectural perimeters such as walls or fountain basins call for precise planning and construction, particularly with ground-level water surfaces, if the desired effect is to be visible. This method requires materials with a low dimensional tolerance (e.g. natural stone or concrete components), elements for precise water feed and drainage, and supporting technology (e.g. pump circulation). › Figs 61 and 62

WATER INFLOW AND OUTFLOW

Each system requires water inflow, for the day-to-day maintenance of the water level, and a water outflow, as well as a bottom outlet, if possible, to completely drain the water installation.

\\ Tip:
The visible surface quality of the water can be controlled by the type of inflow. A method that employs low surface tension feed lines, located deep below the water's surface and above a basin connected upstream, produces a clear, smooth surface. Channels flush with the water's edge, which have a moderate surface tension feed line, make band-like waves and circular waves with a concentric source.

Fig.59:
A grass bank for a low current stream

Fig.60:
A straight, shallow extending gravel bank with scattered heavy rocks

Fig.61:
Hardwearing, curving perimeter made of in situ concrete

Fig.62:
Detail of a ground-level reflecting pool with a finely structured steel edging

Inflow and outflow are the starting and end point of any water design and have to be developed along with the overall concept. Their hydraulic capacity must be made to correspond with the system as a whole, and to operate either independently without the need for a pressurized system, or with a pressurized system using pumps and elevated tanks. These can be completely concealed or clearly visible, and should remain accessible for maintenance work and protected from harmful impurities by a filter system.

Concealed in-
flow and outflow

Concealed systems consist of a pressure hose and a suction hose, which are integrated in a pump system and hidden under the water surface. An additional water basin placed in front of the inflow can slow the speed of water flow in order to control, reduce, or avoid visible swirling on the water's surface. › Fig. 63 With depressurized systems, inflows and outflows can be concealed outside of the water using chutes, channels, and inflows.

›✎

Fig.63:
Still water surface with a barely visible inflow built into the basin floor

Fig.64:
Decorative fountain pipe

Fig.65:
Water source made of fired clay

Fig.66:
Protective grating over a pond spill-
over in the form of a leaf

Visible inflow
and outflow

The possibilities of a visible, and therefore, designable inflow and
outflow system are very diverse. In simple cases, they are designed as a
simple water figure rising from the surface, perhaps as a constant gur-
gle or pulsing geyser. Technical constructions, such as the overflow from
dams, coastal pumping stations, or pumps that have a rough technical
charm can be designed and integrated in a manner that suits this context.
One simple example would be extended water outflow pipes › Fig. 64 made
of cast iron or bronze, decorated or plain, straight or curved. Water can
gush from built elements, natural rock, or processed stones, bowls, chutes,
or steel grating; it can surge over or vanish into them. Finally, the water sources can be collected and designed to enhance this effect, by using
sculptural forms, artificial sculpturally emphasized elements, allegorical

Fig.67:
Outlet in the middle of a reflective pool

figures, fairytale figures, or fountain saints that all spray, squirt, spill and catch water. › Figs 65, 66 and 67

Bottom outlet

For maintenance work and emptying the pool in winter, › Chapter Technical parameters, Winter protection the bottom outlet should be designed as a simple technical element that is barely visible but easy to operate. It can be an outflow unit located at the deepest part of the basin floor that can be opened and closed by a sliding valve, that is, a bilge pump that can also be a part of the entire pump system, or, in smaller installations, a simple standpipe for overflow, which can be completely removed when emptying the basin.

MOVEMENT

Movement influences the visible character of water. Installations with moving water can be classified in three ways: flowing, falling, and rising.

\\ Note:
In connection with the inflow and outflow, quieter water movements and technologically simple solutions can, for the most part, be developed as depressurized along with the natural flow of the water. Lively, swirling water surfaces, in contrast, need enough pressure to propel the water and, hence, the necessary technology.

Fig.68:
Moving water surface in a sculpturally
designed water channel

Fig.69:
A dam creates some turbulence and
different speeds of flow.

Flowing water

Bodies of flowing water like brooks or channels play with water flowing downward from a high position to a lower one. They can be simple channels, a sequence of basins, or a combination of natural or artificial, linear or meandering forms. Channels require permanent water feed and will run dry if this supply is interrupted. It is wise to retain some water with subtle, built-in barriers and hollows in order to keep it active when the system is turned off or if there is a prolonged dry spell.

The amount of water required for an installation can be calculated, using the diameter of the outflow point, the slope, the degree of surface roughness in the channel, and the speed of flow. With uniform slopes, widening the section slows the flow. Narrowing it increases the speed. › Fig. 68 The appearance of waves and whirlpools on the water's surface is influenced by the course of the channels and how frequently it shifts direction, by the speed of flow, existing swells and breaks, and by the surface structure of the section. › Fig. 69

Falling water

Waterfall installations work with free falling volumes of water. For this method, water is collected before an overhang, slowed and retained before flowing over the projection and falling over the edge into water below.

The overhang, edge, and speed of flow determine the water cascade's clarity, constancy, or calmness. › Fig. 70 The more calm, clear, and consistent

Fig.70:
A film of water that increasingly
fragments

a waterfall is intended to be, the more precisely the constant flow of water will have to be calculated, and the more accurately the surface, construction, and horizontal installation of the overhangs and edges will need to be developed. Natural, "wild" waterfalls have moving, turbulent sheets of water and misty spumes. They function with irregular edges, changing currents, and impact stones to enhance the noisy effect. Since it is difficult to predetermine the actual optical effect of falling water, it is best to test-run the installation during the construction phase to make any necessary improvements or adjustments.

\\ Tip:
If a powerful waterfall lands in a still pool of water, the reverberations on the water's surface will continue far out into the water. In order to keep the calm character of the still water, a stone can be placed in the stream, just behind the impact from the falls. This interrupts the visible movement on the water and calms the surface.

Waterfalls, particularly those with precise, clear sheets of water, react sensitively to debris. Even slight water impurities such as leaves are enough to tear the film of water, making its fall irregular. A good location, screens or filters located upstream from the overhang can guard against this problem and keep the flowing water clear and free of impurities.

Rising water

Fountain installations consist of rising jets of water of varying heights and strengths. They can be arranged alone or in groups, and be constant or rhythmic in height and movement. Their individual form results from the specific combination, water pressure, and shape of the fountain nozzles and fixtures. › Fig. 71

Single jet nozzles › Fig. 72 create a clear, wind-resistant, full water jet that can rise as high as 14 m and be pitched at a 15° angle from the vertical. A multi-jet nozzle creates jets of water that fall diverging or merging together. When mounted on a revolving base, the recoiling water creates a rotating, screw-shaped form. Water-saving hollow jet nozzles are used for fountains with an elevation of up to 80 m. Water film nozzles create closed, but wind-sensitive forms like dome-shaped water bells. Fan nozzles produce the impressive, full picture of a large, closed, fan-shaped water spray at a 30° angle. Finger nozzles produce a vertical or diagonal, bizarre, broken sheet of water. If air is added to the nozzles, the spray becomes full of contrast, bubbly, and foamy, with a powerful wind-resistant body. › Fig. 81 Elaborate switching mechanisms and fast pressure valves produce swaying, dancing water shapes.

Mist fountains in outdoor installations are a special form of fountain installations, where water is finely sprayed using high-pressure valves. The fine mist lowers the air temperature, which is pleasantly fresh in summer. It produces constantly changing, fleeting shapes that are playfully

---

\\ Tip:
If the rate of water flow is low, adhesion power will stop a clear stream from forming, and even the transition into a free fall. The water gets "stuck" in the fall, wanders back, or falls in haphazard, broken streams. Carving a draining lip on the underside directly after the edge, for instance in the form of a milled groove in a stone, can avoid this problem.

\\ Note:
It is important to consider the correct size of the basin when designing a fountain, so that water carried by the wind can be collected. The recommended ratio between the height of the stream and the width of the basin is 1:2, and 1:3 in case of strong wind. In tight spaces, this can lead to difficulties with adjacent uses. This can be rectified by correct positioning together with an automatic wind gauge control system.

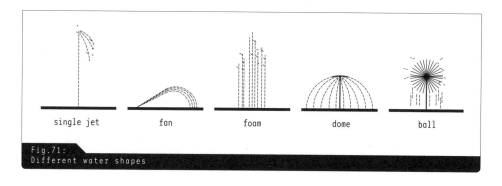

single jet   fan   foam   dome   ball

Fig.71:
Different water shapes

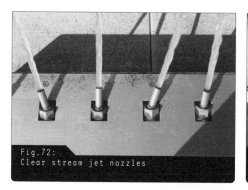

Fig.72:
Clear stream jet nozzles

Fig.73:
Aquatic recreation area with temporary banks of mist

enchanting and fluctuate between transparent and opaque. The installations' fine nozzles make them sensitive to impurities and calciferous water, and their level of water loss depends on wind conditions, and they therefore need a constant water inflow. › Fig. 73

PUMPS AND TECHNOLOGY

The movement of water is the result of balancing differences in height or pressure that is artificially created by pumps, pipe systems, and reservoir tanks.

Pump types

Submersible pumps are placed within the body of water in the middle of the basin to save space, or protected inside a nearby shed. Anchored to a platform, they can float on the surface in the middle of a lake and are used in the design of large fountain installations.

Dry pumps remain outside the water in a separate pump chamber and are connected to a reservoir by cables. Dry pumps are more complex

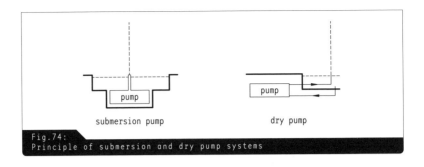

submersion pump   dry pump

Fig.74:
Principle of submersion and dry pump systems

to integrate and therefore more expensive, but can be maintained without great effort, making them more cost-efficient. They are common in large and public installations. › Fig. 74

Installation

Pumps should be enclosed with a protective grille to guard against accidents and should be protected against impurities with a filter and a grit trap. They are operated automatically by a float switch or magnetic switch control and computer programs.

The type and size of the installation and the planned movement and volume of water determine the choice of pump. For smaller, simpler installations, the wide availability of prefabricated solutions is usually sufficient. Pumps greatly affect the running costs of an installation, which makes it advisable to seek advice from specialist engineers and the manufacturer when considering the design.

› 🗋 › 🔎

🗋

\\ Note:
In waterfalls or running water installations without their own reservoirs, pumps at rest collect the otherwise moving water in the last, bottom compartment. The required volumes can be stored in visible ponds or basins, which can be seen in clear fluctuations of water levels, and also require the appropriate dimension and perimeter. Concealed, underground collecting and compensating tanks reduce the visible effect and are therefore preferred for design reasons.

🔎

\\ Example:
Historic installations, such as the animated fountains in Kassel-Wilhelmshöhe's landscape park, Germany, often function using elevated tanks that are kept full by a low, but steady level of pump power, and then emptied as a spectacular event over a specified period of time. With this technique, animated fountains are not in operation at any other time, but are limited to predetermined intervals. In modern installations, pumps are developed for the specific object and allow flexibility, control, and operation round the clock.

LIGHTING

Darkness robs water of its optical power of attraction, quickly turning it into a dark, impenetrable surface. A lighting concept specifically created for the design can animate the water at night and dramatize it with specific lighting.

Outside light sources

Light hitting the surface of water from the outside creates a soft reflection on the otherwise dark plane. The intensity of the reflection depends on the light source's brightness, the distance between the light and the water surface, the color spectrum, and movement on the surface of the water. Colors can also be added by the light source, but they look paler and less saturated when reflected.

Underwater light source

Intense luminosity can be achieved by placing light sources inside the water. They can be located along the basin perimeter, in the soil, or close to fountains. Depending on the brightness of the lighting, the distance to the surrounding fixtures, and the water's transparency, reflections on the basin walls can illuminate the entire body of water. The different angles of refraction emanating from an illuminated body of water with movement on the surface produce a constantly changing structured pattern, and project a play of light and shadow onto the surrounding environment.

Only specific underwater lights or cold lights can be used for underwater lighting concepts. In this procedure, light from an outside projector is directed under the water via glass fibers. Color can be added by using color filters.

PLANTS

Images of water almost always include plants: the water lilies in Monet's garden, a picturesque willow at a pond's edge, the soft, swishing sound of reeds lining a beach. Even architectural designs are willing to interrupt their strict linearity and precise forms by integrating the soft contours and movements of plants.

Their height, density, colors, and leaf structure change during the course of the year. While trees can display their impressive charm in large spaces like parks or landscaped grounds, smaller spaces are characterized in detail mainly by shrubbery.

Choosing a location

Plants will only thrive in a location that suits their individual needs. These habitats are determined by a plant variety's specific needs for light, soil, and water. Trees such as willows or alders are more tolerant than

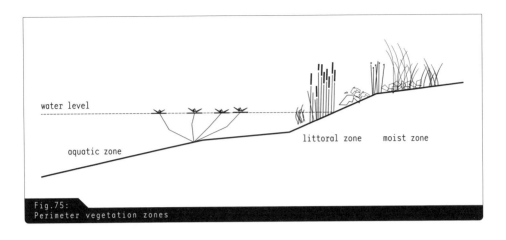

water level

aquatic zone

littoral zone   moist zone

Fig.75:
Perimeter vegetation zones

shrubs, which respond sensitively to changes and fluctuations in the environment.

The habitats of plants can be allocated to different zones according to their respective ideal distance to water. › Fig. 75 Moist zones are located just beyond the water's edge. The capillary effect keeps the ground constantly wet, and occasional flooding is possible. This is a perfect habitat for floral shrubbery and marsh plants, which can tolerate constant moisture. Semi-aquatic plants may grow in water of up to 60 cm deep, depending on their variety. Deeper areas are ideal for plants that are rooted in the soil but have leaves that float on the water's surface; or for floating aquatic plants and underwater plants.

Plants are sensitive to water movement, which can restrict the choice of plant variety, according to the strength of the current. Blades from cane break will bend and underwater plants will be uprooted if the movement of the water is too strong. Water that drops onto the leaves, for example from an animated fountain, can have a magnifying glass effect and produce unsightly burns on the plant.

Growing power   Given the right habitat with the correct nutrients and amount of water, aquatic plants thrive with astounding vitality and growth, changing the appearance of the water design in a short period. Some plant varieties will be suppressed; water surfaces can become completely overgrown. Medium-term plant stability can only be assured if the size of the overall installation is large enough to accommodate the planted area, if there is a nutrient-poor plant substratum, if the vegetation is planted in baskets

Fig.76:
Willows are a symbol for water and
riverbanks in every culture.

Fig.77:
Water lilies in sunken baskets placed
in a geometric reflecting pool

that restrict its growth, and if the installation is regularly maintained.
> **Fig. 77**

The right selection and combination of plants requires moderation in
variety and density, great care and experience, if an attractive, stable, and
visible structure is desired.

> >

WATER QUALITY

Despite the increasing number of aesthetically demanding examples
that focus thematically on pollution, change, and transformation, there are
other cases that present the desired ideal of clear, fresh, and transparent
water. Murky water, algae, or even brackish, foul-smelling bodies of water

\\Tip:
Biological factors affect the natural presence
of plants near water. This has influenced our
visual experience so much that those plants we
often see near water, such as willows of reeds,
have even come to symbolize water. These may
be used strategically as design elements (see
Fig. 76).

\\Note:
Tables 1–3 in the Appendix provide a basic
guide to varieties of water plants. Additional
information and design approaches can be found
in *Basics Designing with Plants* by Regine Ellen
Wöhrle and Hans-Jörg Wöhrle, Birkhäuser Verlag,
Basel 2008, as well as in *Perennials and their
garden habitats* by Richard Hansen and Friedrich
Stahl, Cambridge 1993.

Fig.78:
Thick algae cover the entire surface of the water.

demonstrate not only a lack of biological equilibrium, but also a failed design. › Fig. 78

Biological
equilibrium
Biological equilibrium is a prerequisite for clear, transparent water. It can be achieved only if substrate producers and substrate eaters – plants, animals, and microorganisms – are in proportion to one another. This can be achieved if the water is slightly shaded, if there is water movement that brings about oxygenation, if the body of water is larger, deeper and hence cooler, is not heavily exploited, and has a low animal population.

In closed systems, biological equilibrium requires the water to be changed or cleaned continually by both natural and artificial means, that is electronic or chemical processes.

Natural
cleaning
Larger, natural installations, such as swimming ponds with a balanced proportion of exposed water surface and perimeters with a self-cleaning capacity, almost exclusively use a natural cleaning method. This cleans the water within a constructed wetland that contains reeds, and sometimes cattail, mud rush, or sedges. The plants' roots are a perfect habitat for microorganisms that break down foreign nutrients and harmful substances, supply oxygen to the water, and contribute to cleaning it.

Hybrid systems that support the natural cleaning capacity by mechanically recirculating the water and using sand filters along the edge zones are recommended for installations that are heavily used, such as public swimming ponds.

Artificial
cleaning
Artificial cleaning simulates the natural processes but is concentrated on a small space. In the first mechanical-hydraulic phase, large debris is removed from the water by screens, and fine floating sediments by skimmers, sieves, and crystal-quartz sand filters. In the following chemical phase, the pH of the water is neutralized by adding acidity or leaching with an automatic pH regulator. Bacteria are kept at bay with bactericidal products such as chlorine, which is controversial when used outdoors, or by adding hydrogen peroxide or silver oxide.

Complete technical conditioning is common for architectural installations without vegetation, which except for freshwater, have no natural cleaning capacity. Installations such as aquatic recreation areas that are heavily used require hygienic, high-quality water treatment.

SAFETY

Water has always been both fascinating and threatening. The safety requirements when using water as a design element are therefore very high, to guard against the risk of accidents. The different possible dangers include deep water, entering the water unsupervised, and the underwater technical equipment such as pumps or inlet pipes.

Precautions
Having to integrate safety measures after the installation has been constructed is almost always detrimental to the design. It makes more sense to address these issues during the design phase and to consider the aspect of safety as a part of the overall concept. The most important points to consider include:

_ Controlled access to the water: Closed and accessible banks should be designed clearly so that visitors can easily differentiate between the two. Accessible banks should allow the water to be accessed by ramps, steps, stepping-stones, or handrails.
_ The right water depth: A safe water depth is essential in accessible areas where children play. In water that is already deep, an underwater grating can be installed to create a safe, relatively shallow depth. › Fig. 79

_ Good escape routes out of the water: If there is an accident, it should be easy to leave the water without requiring help from others. This can be achieved by a relatively gentle slope of 1/3 or less, or with steps or ladders.

_ Equipment safety: Technical equipment such as inlet pipes or immersion pumps should be covered with grating to guard against accidents.

WINTER PROTECTION

Depending on the region in question, the cold season, when water freezes and develops a particular aesthetic effect as snow and ice, can encompass up to half the year. Due to the anomaly of water, that is, its capacity to expand up to 10% in volume when frozen, low temperatures pose a threat to a water installation's technical equipment. To protect it, most installations are emptied and closed at the beginning of winter. They look abandoned, gloomy, and unsightly compared to permanent installations. A good design always considers the installation's year-round appearance, taking into account the closed phase (such as winter) from a design and a technical point of view, and developing a suitable design response.

Still water freezes more quickly than moving water. Heating the water and basin, or adding chemicals, can prevent or at least delay the water from freezing, but the high construction and maintenance costs make this solution less attractive.

Installations at risk of frost are usually closed and completely emptied at the beginning of the frost period. During this period, an outlet should be kept open to drain water that accumulates from precipitation, seepage, and condensation, which can also freeze.

Simple constructions can be closed during winter and do not need to be protected. Valuable structures such as fountains with sensitive sculptures and decorative elements are protected mostly by wood casings.

Installations with liners that are sensitive to dryness, such as clay or silt, or that have a dense flora and fauna population remain filled with water during the winter season. There needs to be enough space at the perimeter to allow for the expansion of ice so as to avoid damage to these installations, and the existing closed, water-filled pipes have to be protected against frost. How deeply frost penetrates the soil depends on the local climate. The average frost depth ranges from 0.8 to 1.2 m.

Water plants that have been correctly chosen for the location and its climate will not need additional winter protection. To ensure that the aquatic animals survive, there has to have been an adequate amount of frost-protected water to offer as much habitat as necessary below the ice layer.

The end of the winter season signals an intense period of cleaning, where the protective casing is removed, leaves, mud, and refuse are eliminated, and the luxuriant plants are returned. Before reopening the installation, the equipment is serviced, and the installation is checked for any possible damage.

COST EFFECTIVENESS
Of the three design elements of landscape architecture – vegetation, topography, and water – it is the last that has the greatest long-term influence on cost. The initial costs, however, are not the most significant. Mid-size, artificial water installations and simple constructions cost about the same to build as mounted ones. Even more elaborate animated fountains are relatively reasonable to produce because of their concentrated size.

It is the constant care, maintenance, and repairs that make a water installation costly in the medium term. The economic factor can hinder good designs from being realized, or could mean technically perfect, built installations being closed down because of a lack of finances.

Sustainable designs should therefore try to create a lasting and cohesive design, in terms of cost, during the planning and conception phase. This is possible if existing elements are exploited and designed optimally, and it becomes structurally feasible if the necessary technological standards are lowered, and if the workmanship is good down to the last detail.

Optimizing the concept

Conceptually, solutions that rely on the site and what is locally available are in a better position to make the best use of synergies and cost. Buried brooks can be rediscovered and opened, existing basins used in a new way, or rainwater allowed to playfully run through open channels, or be directed into cisterns and ponds. › Fig. 80

The appropriate standards

› ℗

Greater tolerance in the design and a slight lowering of standards allow water installations to be realized and maintained more easily. This allows for a less expensive integration of natural processes, for example in the case of near-natural swimming ponds that rely on self-cleaning ability, rather than traditional swimming pools that need elaborate and costly technical installations.

Optimizing the construction

In order to avoid the need for subsequent repairs, it is recommended to choose a durable solution over an apparently cost-effective construction. Any possibility of simplifying and reducing repairs and maintenance should be exploited; for example, protecting against excessive amounts of leaves by providing easy accessibility for maintenance, or by calibrating the installation with others belonging to the same operator in order to exploit operational synergies and the availability of spare parts.

℗
\\ Example:
In 2002 in Grossenhain, Germany, the outdoor swimming pool was replaced by a natural swimming pool. 2000 m^2 of regeneration surface is adjacent to 3000 m^2 of swimming pond, which is used by up to 1,800 visitors a day. The natural swimming pool reduced operational costs by 40% compared to conventional swimming pools.

Fig.80:
A water basin that collects rainwater
and has vegetation and a wooden deck
form the focal point of a public square.

Fig.81:
Water Block in front of the Louvre

With artificial installations, it is important to note:

_ that the water basin should be as shallow as possible so as to mini-mize the cost of filling and replacing water;
_ that pumps should be installed individually according to the cor-rect requirements in order to optimize energy and water use;
_ that animated fountains should not be located in windy passages so as to avoid excessive water loss;
_ that thorough winter protection measures will guard against dam-age to technical equipment.

With "natural" installations

_ the body of water should be as large as possible so as to avoid warming too quickly;
_ vegetation should only be planted in baskets to contain their growth;
_ fish should not be introduced because the nutrients they bring en-courage the growth of algae.

IN CONCLUSION

Water is an essential, almost unavoidable, element when designing outdoor spaces. Its symbolic character, vivacity, its unique emotional quality, and immanent diversity provide the opportunity to develop a suitable but distinctive overall concept with visual poetry. Water designs grab people's attention – how it functions naturally, how one feels it work, and how it moves the observer's emotions. Contact with water triggers a deeply rooted reflection in relation to the overall context, a response to the uniqueness of the site, accuracy of material, and quality of workmanship as a basis for a design's success.

Water is freedom. Within the boundaries of the physical specifications, there is an almost infinite amount of room for creativity. Water generates curiosity and the desire to experiment. It offers long-lasting appeal and is always surprising. This text aims to be an introduction – an incentive to observe, a call to experiment, and an encouragement to explore the path less trodden.

APPENDIX

AQUATIC PLANTS

The table below provides an overview of suitable aquatic plants and can serve as an introductory guideline to planting vegetation.

Tab.1:
Selection of shrubs for moist zones

Variety	English name	Exposure to sun	Height	Bloom time (month)	Bloom color
Ajuga reptans	Common bugleweed	Half-shade	10–20 cm	IV–V	Blue
Caltha palustris	Marsh marigold	Sun to half-shade	30 cm	III–IV	Golden yellow
Cardamine pratensis	Cuckoo flower	Half-shade to shade	30 cm	IV–VI	Lilac-pink
Carex elata "Bowles Golden"	Bowles' golden sedge	Sun to half-shade	60 cm	VI	Brown
Carex grayi	Grey's sedge	Sun to shade	30–60 cm	VII–VIII	Green-brown
Darmera peltata	Indian rhubarb	Sun to half-shade	80 cm	IV–V	Pink
Eupatorium species	Gravel root	Sun to shade	80–200 cm	VII–VIII	Dark pink
Filipendula ulmaria	Meadowsweet	Sun to half-shade	120 cm	VI–VIII	Cream
Frittilaria meleagris	Checkered lily	Half-shade	20–30 cm	IV–V	Violet
Geum rivale	Water avens	Sun to half-shade	30 cm	IV–V	Golden brown
Gunnera tinctoria	Giant rhubarb	Sun	150 cm	IX	Red
Hemerocallis wild species	Daylily	Sun–half-shade	40–90 cm	V–VIII	Yellow/orange
Iris sibirica	Siberian iris	Sun to half-shade	40–90 cm	V–VI	Violet
Leucojum vernum	Spring snowflake	Half-shade to sun	20–40 cm	II–IV	White
Ligularia species and hybrids	Ragwort	Sun to half-shade	80–200 cm	VI–IX	Yellow/orange
Lysimachia clethroides	Gooseneck loose-strife	Sun to half-shade	70–100 cm	VII–VIII	White
Lythrum salicaria	Purple loose-strife	Sun to half-shade	80–140 cm	VII–IX	Violet
Myosotis palustris	Water forget-me-not	Sun to half-shade	30 cm	V–IX	Blue
Primula species and hybrids	Primrose	Half-shade to shade	40–60 cm	II–VIII	White/yellow/pink-red/ orange/ lilac-violet
Tradescantia-Andersoniana hybrids	Andersons Spiderwood	Sun	40–60 cm	VI–VIII	Blue/violet/white/carmine
Trollius euro-paeus/Trollius hybrids	Globe-flower	Sun to half-shade	40–70 cm	IV–VI	Yellow/orange
Veronica longifolia	Garden speedwell	Sun	50–120 cm	VII–VIII	Blue

Variety	English name	Exposure to sun	Water depth	Height	Bloom time	Bloom color
Acorus calamus	Sweet flag	Sun to half-shade	0–30 cm	to 120 cm	V–VI	Yellow
Alisma plantago-aquatica	Water plantain	Sun to half-shade	5–30 cm	40–80 cm	VI–VIII	White
Butomus umbellatus	Flowering rush	Sun to half-shade	10–40 cm	100 cm	VI–VIII	Pink
Calla palustris	Water arum	Sun to half-shade	0–15 cm	to 40 cm	V–VII	White-yellow
Caltha palustris	Marsh marigold	Sun to shade	0–30 cm	to 30 cm	IV–VI	Yellow
Carex pseudocyperus	Cypress-like sedge	Sun	0–20 cm	80 cm	VI–VII	–
Equisetum fluviatale	Swamp horsetail	Sun to half-shade	0–5 cm	20–150 cm	–	–
Hippuris vulgaris	Common marestail	Sun to half-shade	10–40 cm	40 cm	V–VIII	Green
Iris pseudocorus	Yellow flag	Sun to shade	0–30 cm	60–80 cm	V–VIII	Yellow
Phragmites australis "Variegatus"	Common reed (yellow striped variety)	Sun	0–20 cm	120–150 cm	VII–IX	Brownish-red
Pontederia cordata	Pickerel weed	Shade to half-shade	0–30 cm	50–60 cm	VI–VIII	Blue
Sagittaria sagittifolia	Arrowhead	Sun	10–40 cm	30–60 cm	VI–VIII	White
Scirpus lacustris	Bulrush	Sun to half-shade	10–60 cm	to 120 cm	VII–VIII	Brown
Sparganium erectum	Bur-reed	Sun to half-shade	0–30 cm	100 cm	VII–VIII	Green
Typha angustifolia	Narrow leaf cattail	Sun	0–50 cm	150–200 cm	VII–VIII	Reddish brown spadices
Typha minima	Miniature cattail	Sun	0–40 cm	50–60 cm	VI–VII	Brown bells
Veronica beccabunga	Brooklime	Sun to half-shade	0–20 cm	40–60 cm	V–IX	Blue

Variety	English name	Exposure to sun	Height	Bloom time	Bloom color
Callitriche palustris	Common water-wort	Sun to half-shade	10–30 cm	–	–
Ceratophyllum demersum	Hornwort	Sun to half-shade	30–100 cm	Summer	Not visible
Elodea canadensis	Canadian pond-weed	Sun	20–100 cm	–	–
Hydrocharis morsus-ranae	European frog-bit	Sun to half-shade	from 20 cm	VI–VIII	White
Myriophyllum verticillatum	Myriad leaf	Sun to half-shade	30 cm	VI–VIII	Pink
Lemna minor	Duckweed	Sun	from 20 cm	–	–
Lemna trisulca	Star duckweed	Sun	from 20 cm	–	–
Nuphar lutea	Yellow water-lily	Sun to shade	40–100 cm	VI–VIII	Yellow
Nymphaea alba	White water-lily	Sun	60–100 cm	V–VIII	White
Nymphaea-Hybriden, e.g. "Anna Epple", "Charles de Meurville", "Marliacea Albida", "Maurica Laydeker"	Water-lilies: hybrids	Sun	40–60 cm	VI–IX	Pink/ burgundy/ pure white/ purple
Nymphaea odorata "Rosennymphe"	Fragrant water-lily	Sun	40–60 cm	VI–IX	Pink
Nymphaea tuberosa "Pöstlingberg"	Tuberous water-lily	Sun	60–80 cm	VI–IX	White
Nymphoides peltata	Yellow floating-heart	Sun to half-shade	40–50 cm	VII–VIII	Yellow
Potamogeton natans	Broad-leafed pondweed	Sun to half-shade	40–100 cm	VI–IX	White
Ranunculus aquatilis	Water crowfoot	Sun	30 cm	VI–VIII	White
Stratiotes aloides	Water soldier	Sun to half-shade	30–100 cm	VI–VIII	White
Trapa natans	Water chestnut	Sun	40–120 cm	VI–VII	Light blue
Utricularia vulgaris	Bladderwort	Sun to half-shade	20–40 cm	VII–VIII	Yellow

LITERATURE

Alejandro Bahamón: *Water Features*, Loft Publications, Barcelona 2006

David Bennett: *Concrete*, Birkhäuser Verlag, Basel 2001

Bert Bielefeld, Sebastian El khouli: *Basics Design Ideas*, Birkhäuser Verlag, Basel 2007

Ulrike Brandi, Christoph Geissmar-Brandi: *Lightbook, The Practice of Lighting Design*, Birkhäuser Verlag, Basel/Boston 2001

Francis Ching: *Architecture: Form, Space and Order*, Van Nostrand Reinhold, London/New York 1979

Christian Cajus Lorenz Hirschfeld: *Theory of Garden Art*, University of Pennsylvania Press, Philadelphia, PA 2001

Paul Cooper: *The New Tech Garden,* Octopus, London 2001

Herbert Dreiseitl, Dieter Grau, Karl Ludwig: *New Waterscapes*, Birkhäuser Verlag, Basel 2005

Edition Topos: *Water, Designing with Water, From Promenades to Water Features*, Birkhäuser Verlag, Basel 2003

Renata Giovanardi: *Carlo Scarpa e l'aqua*, Cicero editore, Venice 2006

Richard Hansen, Friedrich Stahl: *Perennials and Their Garden Habitats*, Cambridge University Press, Cambridge 1993

Teiji Itoh: *The Japanese Gardens*, Yale University Press, New Haven/London 1972

Hans Loidl, Stefan Bernhard: *Opening Spaces*, Birkhäuser Verlag, Basel 2003

Gilly Love: *Water in the Garden*, Aquamarine, London 2001

Ernst Neufert: *Architects' Data*, Blackwell Science Publishers, Malden, MA 2000

OASE Fountain Technologie 2007/08, http://www.oase-livingwater.com/

George Plumptre: *The Water Garden*, Thames & Hudson, London 2003

TOPOS 59 – Water, Design and Management, Callwey Verlag, Munich 2007

Udo Weilacher: *Syntax of Landscape*, Birkhäuser Verlag, Basel 2007

Stephen Woodhams: *Portfolio of Contemporary Gardens*, Quadrille, London 1999

THE AUTHOR

Axel Lohrer, Dipl.-Ing. (FH), practicing landscape architect and partner at lohrer.hochrein landschaftsarchitekten in Munich and Magdeburg.

Series editor: Bert Bielefeld
Editor for this volume: Cornelia Bott
Conception: Bert Bielefeld, Annette Gref
Layout and Cover design: Muriel Comby
Translation from German into English: Laura Bruce
English Copy editing: Monica Buckland

Library of Congress Control Number: 2008925387

Bibliographic information published by the German National Library
The German National Library lists this publication in the Deutsche Nationalbibliografie; detailed bibliographic data are available on the Internet at http://dnb.d-nb.de.

This book is also available in a German (ISBN 978-3-7643-8660-3) and a French (ISBN 978-3-7643-8661-0) language edition.

© 2008 Birkhäuser Verlag AG
Basel · Boston · Berlin
P.O. Box 133, CH-4010 Basel, Switzerland
Part of Springer Science+Business Media

Printed on acid-free paper produced from chlorine-free pulp. TCF ∞
Printed in Germany

ISBN 978-3-7643-8662-7
9 8 7 6 5 4 3 2 1   www.birkhauser.ch

Also available from Birkhäuser:

Design
Basics Design and Living
Jan Krebs
978-3-7643-7647-5

Basics Design Ideas
Bert Bielefeld, Sebastian El khouli
978-3-7643-8112-7

Basics Design Methods
Kari Jormakka
978-3-7643-8463-0

Basics Materials
M. Hegger, H. Drexler, M. Zeumer
978-3-7643-7685-7

Fundamentals of Presentation
Basics CAD
Jan Krebs
978-3-7643-8109-7

Basics Modelbuilding
Alexander Schilling
978-3-7643-7649-9

Basics Technical Drawing
Bert Bielefeld, Isabella Skiba
978-3-7643-7644-4

Construction
Basics Facade Apertures
Roland Krippner, Florian Musso
978-3-7643-8466-1

Basics Loadbearing Systems
Alfred Meistermann
978-3-7643-8107-3

Basics Masonry Construction
Nils Kummer
978-3-7643-7645-1

Basics Roof Construction
Tanja Brotrück
978-3-7643-7683-3

Basics Timber Construction
Ludwig Steiger
978-3-7643-8102-8

Building Services / Building Physics
Basics Room Conditioning
Oliver Klein, Jörg Schlenger
978-3-7643-8664-1

Professional Practice
Basics Project Planning
Hartmut Klein
978-3-7643-8469-2

Basics Site Management
Lars-Phillip Rusch
978-3-7643-8104-2

Basics Tendering
Tim Brandt, Sebastian Th. Franssen
978-3-7643-8110-3

Urbanism
Basics Urban Building Blocks
Thorsten Bürklin, Michael Peterek
978-3-7643-8460-9

Landscape Architecture
Basics Designing with Plants
Regine Ellen Wöhrle, Hans-Jörg Wöhrle
978-3-7643-8659-7

BIRKHÄUSER

Available at your bookshop or at
www.birkhauser.ch

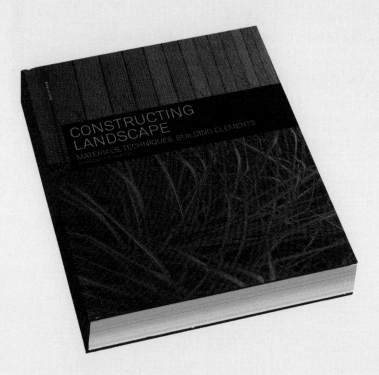